Daily Delights

Thoughts of Advent

Daily Delights

Thoughts of Advent

Delight in Him!
Jacqueline
Heider

Jacqueline C. Heider

Daily Delights: Thoughts of Advent

Copyright © 2016 by Jacqueline C. Heider

All rights reserved. This book or any portion thereof may not be reproduced or used in any manner whatsoever without the express written permission of the publisher except for the use of brief quotations in a book review.

For permission requests write to:

contacts@jacquelineheider.com

Printed in the United States of America

First Printing, 2016

ISBN: 978-1539428848

Scripture quotations are from the ESV® Bible (The Holy Bible, English Standard Version®), copyright © 2001 by Crossway, a publishing ministry of Good News Publishers. Used by permission. All rights reserved.

Special thanks to Tracey Drake, Laura Starnes, Dr. David H. McKinley & Warren Baptist Church, Augusta, GA

Dedication

To my precious children, Austen, JD and Leanna,
who love the season of Jesus' birth
as much as I do!

The merriest of Christmases to you my loves!!

Momma

Contents

Acknowledgments

My parents instilled a love for the Christmas season in me from the time I was three months old. The tradition of going to MaMa's house is forever ingrained in my heart and mind. From the lighting of the Advent wreath, to singing carols around the piano, to reading the story of Christ's birth, they lovingly taught me traditions of the season that caused me to long for the celebration of Jesus' birth.

Thank you, Momma and Daddy, for always making Christmas the most wonderful time of the year for your little girl!

I love you both more than words can convey.

Foreward

This Christmas devotional is meant to help us experience the joy and peace of Jesus' presence throughout the season of Advent. So often we get caught up in the hustle and bustle, the to-dos, the lists, the hoopla of it all. My prayer is that this little book will ready our hearts for His coming and steady our minds on the wonderful gift of His presence.

I pray you will be surrounded by the presence of Jesus this season. Blessings to you!

Jacqueline

December 1
Twisting & Turning

Genesis 3:1-7
Now the serpent was more crafty than any other beast of the field that the LORD God had made. He said to the woman, "Did God actually say, 'You shall not eat of any tree in the garden'?" And the woman said to the serpent, "We may eat of the fruit of the trees in the garden, but God said, 'You shall not eat of the fruit of the tree that is in the midst of the garden, neither shall you touch it, lest you die.'" But the serpent said to the woman, "You will not surely die. For God knows that when you eat of it your eyes will be opened, and you will be like God, knowing good and evil." So when the woman saw that the tree was good for food, and that it was a delight to the eyes, and that the tree was to be desired to make one wise, she took of its fruit and ate, and she also gave some to her husband who was with her, and he ate. Then the eyes of both were opened, and they knew that they were naked. And they sewed fig leaves together and made themselves loincloths.

Twisting and turning, that's what the crafty serpent is so very good at, isn't he? "Did God actually say ..." Those were the serpent's words, and in that moment, sin entered into the world.

And then … then their eyes were opened and all changed. Naked and ashamed—because of sin, because of fear, because of self-righteousness—all was lost. But not forever. God had a plan then, just as He does now. His plan? Jesus. Yes, Jesus. He was the answer then, and He is the answer today.

Are you in need of an answer today? The answer is Jesus. Call on Him and allow Him to cover your shame, your sin, your fear, your doubts, your everything. Jesus. The reason for the season. Jesus. The answer to your everything.

Today's Prayer

Precious Jesus, You are the answer to every question. I praise You today for the salvation that is found in You. Thank You for seeing my need for a Savior even before I was born. I give you ________ today and ask You to get me through. Please do not allow the serpent to twist the words you have spoken to me and make me live in doubt, fear, or failure. I ask You to purify my heart of sin and prepare me for the celebration of Your birth. In Your most holy name I pray, amen.

Prepare My Heart

Today, write a note of encouragement to someone who needs to know Jesus.

December 2
The Sound of the Lord

Genesis 3:8-13
And they heard the sound of the LORD God walking in the garden in the cool of the day, and the man and his wife hid themselves from the presence of the LORD God among the trees of the garden. But the LORD God called to the man and said to him, "Where are you?" And he said, "I heard the sound of you in the garden, and I was afraid, because I was naked, and I hid myself." He said, "Who told you that you were naked? Have you eaten of the tree of which I commanded you not to eat?" The man said, "The woman whom you gave to be with me, she gave me fruit of the tree, and I ate." Then the LORD God said to the woman, "What is this that you have done?" The woman said, "The serpent deceived me, and I ate."

The sound of the Lord, what a wonderful sound! Whether in times of trouble, sorrow, sin, or shame, times of delight and joy, anticipation, or adventure—the sound of the Lord drawing near laces the ear with sweetness.

And in that moment, in the beginning, God walked to the first man and the first woman to rescue them from the deceiver. He came. He showed up. He arrived. And what welcome did He receive? Fear.

They were afraid. They knew what had been done, the sin and deception that had taken place.

But God arrived anyway. The sound of the Lord echoed in the garden and all changed. Yes, sin had entered into the world, and by its side stood death, decay, and defeat. Those were the sounds that crashed and clanged through the night. But love would halt the sounds of death and make joyful the strains of Jesus' advent—His coming. The love of God would make a way.

Will you give thanks for His coming today? Will you listen for the sound of the Lord in the loud, angry madness of the season? Listen closely for His coming. Be ready. He is the reason. He will come and rescue once again those who love Him. Don't be afraid. Listen! It's the sound of the Lord's coming.

Today's Prayer

Precious Jesus, thank You for coming. Thank You for rescuing me so long ago, long before I even came to be. Thank You for coming to me today. I yearn to hear and see and feel Your presence in the day-to-day madness. It brings me great joy and peace. Will You give me a sense of Your presence as I travel throughout my day? You are my delight, and I love You, Jesus, amen.

Prepare My Heart

Today, listen to the sounds of the season—carols, bells, the laughter of children, the cry of a baby. Be quiet and listen.

December 3
When God Calls Your Name

Genesis 22:1-8
After these things God tested Abraham and said to him, "Abraham!" And he said, "Here I am." He said, "Take your son, your only son Isaac, whom you love, and go to the land of Moriah, and offer him there as a burnt offering on one of the mountains of which I shall tell you." So Abraham rose early in the morning, saddled his donkey, and took two of his young men with him, and his son Isaac. And he cut the wood for the burnt offering and arose and went to the place of which God had told him. On the third day Abraham lifted up his eyes and saw the place from afar. Then Abraham said to his young men, "Stay here with the donkey; I and the boy will go over there and worship and come again to you." And Abraham took the wood of the burnt offering and laid it on Isaac his son. And he took in his hand the fire and the knife. So they went both of them together. And Isaac said to his father Abraham, "My father!" And he said, "Here I am, my son." He said, "Behold, the fire and the wood, but where is the lamb for a burnt offering?" Abraham said, "God will provide for himself the lamb for a burnt offering, my son." So they went both of them together.

When God calls your name, what is your response? Is it a zealous, *Here I am*? Especially with regard to a sacrifice, would your response be eager? Would mine?

A sacrifice, a burnt offering made unto the Lord, these became necessary after the garden. Why? We have a holy and perfect God, that's why. His presence embodies holiness. It is only consecrated sacrifices and offerings that make us acceptable, not anything we do on our own. We are made from dust, born with a propensity to sin. But God made a way then, a foreshadowing of what was to come, a foreshadowing of His "advent." Abraham alluded to God's coming provision when he said, "God will provide for himself the lamb for a burnt offering, my son." God did provide a way for Abraham's son that day. But one day it would be God's Son who would become the sacrificial lamb. The long awaited, perfect, holy, and complete provision would make His appearing and fulfill His purpose. For now, they would settle for sacrificial lambs, goats, and doves, but in the fullness of time, Jesus would arrive and say, "I AM is here."

Today's Prayer

God, thank You for the provision of Your Son, Jesus, the great I AM, the King of kings, the Lord of lords, Man of sorrows, Lamb of God, Holy One of Israel. What a privilege it is to offer myself to You as a living sacrifice daily! Help me open myself up to You this day completely. Cause me to hold nothing back from You, Lord. Help me say, "Here I am." These things I ask in Jesus' name, amen.

Prepare My Heart

Today, give something away that is precious to you. Offer it as a sacrifice of praise to the Lord.

December 4
King of Your Heart

Genesis 22:9-14

When they came to the place of which God had told him, Abraham built the altar there and laid the wood in order and bound Isaac his son and laid him on the altar, on top of the wood. Then Abraham reached out his hand and took the knife to slaughter his son. But the angel of the LORD called to him from heaven and said, "Abraham, Abraham!" And he said, "Here I am." He said, "Do not lay your hand on the boy or do anything to him, for now I know that you fear God, seeing you have not withheld your son, your only son, from me." And Abraham lifted up his eyes and looked, and behold, behind him was a ram, caught in a thicket by his horns. And Abraham went and took the ram and offered it up as a burnt offering instead of his son. So Abraham called the name of that place, "The LORD will provide"; as it is said to this day, "On the mount of the LORD it shall be provided."

Who is king of your heart today? This test that God gave to Abraham demolished any possible idol that had seeped into the deep recesses of his being. This test screamed at Abraham and caused him to choose—his son or his God. Abraham chose wisely. With faith and faithfulness he chose the Lord, Jehovah-jireh, "The LORD will provide."

As Abraham reached up to make the deadly descent that would strike and kill his beloved son, the Lord reached down and made His provision. Do you see the beauty of such love? And He did the same for us. He reached down from Heaven and placed a beautiful Baby in a manger for you and me. A Baby who would later experience the painful striking blows of nails, and whips, and swords. From a cradle to a cross, God's provision, rich in love and abundant in grace, came down from heaven and crushed our sin. He had no one on His mind but you and me when He endured that shame and guilt. Nothing crowded us out of His heart.

What is crowding Jehovah out of your heart and mind this season? Will you make Jesus King of your heart and allow nothing to reign supreme in your life but Him?

Today's Prayer

Jehovah, great and mighty King, Lord and Master of all, thank You for Your love, grace, and mercy. Thank You for reaching down from Heaven and providing for my needs. My heart's desire is for You to be my everything, my all-consuming passion. Don't allow me to take my focus off of You this season. Presents, people, and projects should be secondary to You. Help me make You my priority each day. In Jesus' name, amen.

Prepare My Heart

Today, fast from something—a habit, a TV show, a meal, technology. Spend that time meditating on the goodness of your King.

December 5
The Blessing of Covenant

Genesis 22:15-21

And the angel of the LORD called to Abraham a second time from heaven and said, "By myself I have sworn, declares the LORD, because you have done this and have not withheld your son, your only son, I will surely bless you, and I will surely multiply your offspring as the stars of heaven and as the sand that is on the seashore. And your offspring shall possess the gate of his enemies, and in your offspring shall all the nations of the earth be blessed, because you have obeyed my voice."

More blessings than the grains on the shore, offspring that outnumber the stars—this was Abraham's reward, the beginning of the earthly family line of Jesus.

Abraham had passed the test of faithfulness and obedience, and in doing so God's promise to bless Him would be accomplished. There would be much wandering and turmoil, many years of waiting for the Messiah, but God's promise was sure because God was and is sure. He is the Faithful One, the Keeper of the Covenant.

Covenant. I love that word. How can one word bring such depth of feeling, confidence, and blessed assurance? Because God's name is behind covenant. The covenant of God is not a possibility, and it isn't a probability. The covenant of God is a certainty, and it is the saved saint's reality. God cannot break His covenant and when He cuts covenant and blood spills, His protection, His love, and His presence become a shield for the redeemed.

Today's Prayer

Covenant Keeper, I praise You today. Jesus, my Savior, the covenant You made secured and saved me. Thank You. Keep me ever mindful of our covenant, Lord. As Advent draws nearer, fill my heart with the longing for your second appearing. For when You come again, I will see You face-to-face and be made into Your likeness. Longing for more of You today, Jesus, amen.

Prepare My Heart

Today, take a few minutes in the midst of your day to write down a list of your blessings. Pray and thank God for these precious gifts.

December 6

Walk In the Light

Isaiah 9:2-5

The people who walked in darkness have seen a great light; those who dwelt in a land of deep darkness, on them has light shone. You have multiplied the nation; you have increased its joy they rejoice before you as with joy at the harvest, as they are glad when they divide the spoil. For the yoke of his burden, and the staff for his shoulder, the rod of his oppressor, you have broken as on the day of Midian. For every boot of the tramping warrior in battle tumult and every garment rolled in blood will be burned as fuel for the fire.

Darkness is all around, but the light that shines forth through Jesus always makes a way for the people of God. Focus on the Light. Rejoice in the Light. Trust in the Light. Rest in the Light. Give your burdens to the Burden-bearer and allow Him to fight the oppressor. Sin no longer reigns. The Messiah, Jesus, He came to earth as a baby, the Prince of Peace, but He reigns as King of kings and Lord of lords. Walk in the light of His presence today!

Today's Prayer

Jesus, You are the Light of the World. There is no darkness in You. Conquering sin was Your assignment, and You fulfilled Your mission. Thank You for Your extravagant love. As I reflect on who You are, cause me to desire only things that are sinless like You. I love You, Lord, amen.

Prepare My Heart

Sometime today, go into a room, light a candle and turn off all of the lights. Sit in the stillness of the dim room and focus on the light. Find rest and delight in Jesus, the Light of the World, today.

December 7
Secure Shoulders

Isaiah 9:6-7

For to us a child is born, to us a son is given; and the government shall be upon his shoulder, and his name shall be called Wonderful Counselor, Mighty God, Everlasting Father, Prince of Peace. Of the increase of his government and of peace there will be no end, on the throne of David and over his kingdom, to establish it and to uphold it with justice and with righteousness from this time forth and forevermore. The zeal of the LORD of hosts will do this.

Upon His shoulders—what a secure place to rest—the shoulders of a Baby who would become righteousness and justice. The One who would establish His kingdom and be born into hearts who would believe. And although sinless, He understands all of our temptations. Although strong and mighty, He understands our weaknesses and heaps grace upon grace on our lives. He is indeed our Wonderful Counselor, our Mighty God, our Everlasting Father, and our Prince of Peace.

Today's Prayer

Oh Jesus, You are wonderful! Thank You for resting me on Your shoulders when I need to be carried. Thank You for the wisdom, power, and peace that come from You. As I worship You today, help me stay focused on Your Advent, Your coming. Show me someone I can help today. What would you have me shoulder for them? Help me be a blessing to someone today. I love You, Lord, amen.

Prepare My Heart

Find someone who needs help with something today. A chore, an errand, a financial or physical need, whomever God puts in your path to help, shoulder a burden for someone. Be the hands and feet of Jesus!

December 8
Something About that Name

Isaiah 11:1-2
There shall come forth a shoot from the stump of Jesse, and a branch from his roots shall bear fruit. And the Spirit of the LORD shall rest upon him, the Spirit of wisdom and understanding, the Spirit of counsel and might, the Spirit of knowledge and the fear of the LORD.

“There shall come forth.” These words prophesied so long ago, full of promise, hope, wisdom, and peace.

“There shall come forth.” Someone so full of the spirit, so full of truth, so full of power and strength—full! Abundant, complete, all-sufficient, all-encompassing, all-surpassing, all-knowing—Jesus.

Plentiful, abounding, lavished—Jesus—the fullness of God, would come forth and in Him all would be complete, satisfied, overflowing.

Jesus! One word changed all things for all time. He, the King of kings, the Holy One. “He shall come forth.”

Today's Prayer

Jesus, Jesus, Jesus. There is something about that name. Jesus, You are to be praised. I anticipate Your coming this season. You are the gift of Christmas. You are more than enough. You are more. You are mine. Thank You for coming. Thank You for coming for me. Thank You for saving me and for loving me even though I am often unloveable. Thank You. In my Savior's name, amen.

Prepare My Heart

Speak the name of Jesus often today. Thank Him. Praise Him. Tell others about this most miraculous and meaningful gift of Christmas.

December 9
He Shall Be Your Peace

Micah 5:2-5
But you, O Bethlehem Ephrathah, who are too little to be among the clans of Judah, from you shall come forth for me one who is to be ruler in Israel, whose coming forth is from of old, from ancient days. Therefore he shall give them up until the time when she who is in labor has given birth; then the rest of his brothers shall return to the people of Israel. And he shall stand and shepherd his flock in the strength of the LORD, in the majesty of the name of the LORD his God. And they shall dwell secure, for now he shall be great to the ends of the earth. And he shall be their peace.

He shall be our peace. Jesus, our peace, the loving and kind Shepherd of our souls. God, born Baby, completely holy, perfect, and sinless; He would come in the humble, quiet, peaceful night and usher in calm. Calm. Isn't that something we all desire? The very word makes my heart rate begin to slow, my breathing relax, my mind quiet. Thank You for calm, Jesus.

But not only peace and calm, this Baby would bring security. To those who believe upon His name, He would vow to protect, uphold, and secure. What majestic promises! What assurance! Thank You,

Jesus, for coming forth and in Your coming, fulfilling Your Word, the promise of sure and secure salvation.

Today's Prayer

Security is important to me, Lord. Thank You for making me secure in Jesus. Thank You for fulfilling that promise and all of Your promises. I am grateful for the peace that comes from knowing and trusting You. I am grateful that You shepherd me through times, both good and bad. Thank You for always being with me. Help me remain mindful of the reality of Your presence as I walk through this day with a heart of calm and a mind filled with peace. In Jesus' name, amen.

Prepare My Heart

We find peace in prayer because in prayer we are never more near to our Lord. Throughout your day, set aside four to five times to pause and pray for one minute. Praise God for fifteen seconds, thank Him for fifteen seconds, use fifteen seconds to confess your sins, and spend the last fifteen seconds asking for Jesus' help and guidance for that portion of your day. Repeat this multiple times throughout the day. Enjoy the peace of Jesus' presence as you pray.

December 10

Joy in the Son

Habakkuk 3:17-19

Though the fig tree should not blossom, nor fruit be on the vines, the produce of the olive fail and the fields yield no food, the flock be cut off from the fold and there be no herd in the stalls, yet I will rejoice in the LORD; I will take joy in the God of my salvation. God, the LORD, is my strength; he makes my feet like the deer's; he makes me tread on my high places.

Oh the joy that comes from the Lord! No matter the circumstance, the trials, the highs or lows, there is always room for joy where Jesus resides. To take delight in Him is to remember the salvation that He was born to bring. Rejoice!

No matter your circumstance, your joy can be complete. Why? Because joy is found in Jesus and as a believer you are complete in Him. There is nothing under the sun that can bring you more delight, more joy, more satisfaction than Jesus, God's one and only Son.

Today's Prayer

Giver of joy, Author of salvation, I praise You on this tenth day of Advent. Thank You for giving me an understanding of who You are. The truths You have shared with me, the lessons you have taught me, and the things I have experienced with You have given me the tools necessary to walk out my faith in every day, real life circumstances. Help me find joy in Your presence today. In Jesus' name, amen.

Prepare My Heart

Take time to rejoice in the God of your salvation today! Sing, praise, take delight. Celebrate the King of your heart!

December 11
God With Us

Isaiah 7:14
Therefore the Lord himself will give you a sign. Behold, the virgin shall conceive and bear a son, and shall call his name Immanuel.

Immanuel, God with us! He is with us! What comfort and joy come from these words! God is with us at all times in all circumstances. He is our Omnipresent God.

The Son of Promise, born to a virgin. The Son of Promise, Savior to His people. The Son of Promise, love in a manger, hope for the nations, light of the world.

Today's Prayer

Jesus, light of the world, You came and You are coming again. I praise You for Your coming, for Your living, for Your dying, for Your promised return, and for Your promise to carry me through times good and bad. I love You, Lord, amen.

Prepare My Heart

Spend time reading God's Word today, looking at the many promises of God He has given to believers.

December 12
Walking with Him

Luke 1:5-7
In the days of Herod, king of Judea, there was a priest named Zechariah, of the division of Abijah. And he had a wife from the daughters of Aaron, and her name was Elizabeth. And they were both righteous before God, walking blamelessly in all the commandments and statutes of the Lord. But they had no child, because Elizabeth was barren, and both were advanced in years.

Righteous before God, Zechariah and Elizabeth walked blamelessly before the Lord. They were God-fearing, obedient believers; yet they had disappointments and sorrows. Their particular sorrow? No baby. Elizabeth was barren and much too old to have a baby at such an advanced age.

Somehow, though, Zechariah and Elizabeth were able to keep their faith in God. They continued to be righteous before the Lord. They continued to place their faith and hope in the One, true God.

In whom or what do you place your hope? Have you been waiting for something for a long time with no answer? Delight in Jesus, the Promised One!

Choose to focus on the Lord and obey Him in all things. Make this season all about Him!

Today's Prayer

Lord, You are faithful! Thank You for keeping Your promises. Thank You for making provisions for me daily. Help me obey You today. Help me see things through Your eyes—the eyes of the One who works miracles! In Jesus' name, amen.

Prepare My Heart

Take a brief walk outside today. Talk to the Lord as you walk and enjoy the lovely Christmas décor. After your walk, warm up inside with a hot cup of cocoa or cider.

December 13

Fear Not

Luke 1:8-17

Now while he was serving as priest before God when his division was on duty, according to the custom of the priesthood, he was chosen by lot to enter the temple of the Lord and burn incense. And the whole multitude of the people were praying outside at the hour of incense. And there appeared to him an angel of the Lord standing on the right side of the altar of incense. And Zechariah was troubled when he saw him, and fear fell upon him. But the angel said to him, "Do not be afraid, Zechariah, for your prayer has been heard, and your wife Elizabeth will bear you a son, and you shall call his name John. And you will have joy and gladness, and many will rejoice at his birth, for he will be great before the Lord. And he must not drink wine or strong drink, and he will be filled with the Holy Spirit, even from his mother's womb. And he will turn many of the children of Israel to the Lord their God, and he will go before him in the spirit and power of Elijah, to turn the hearts of the fathers to the children, and the disobedient to the wisdom of the just, to make ready for the Lord a people prepared."

Do not fear! Calm down! These words spoken by the angel Gabriel were meant to extinguish Zechariah's fear. Staring into the face of the celestial being would have been cause for alarm, don't you think? Then the news, "Your wife is going to have a baby." After all these years, I really can't blame Zechariah for doubting.

When the angel appeared, Zechariah was standing at the Altar of Incense in the temple just outside of the Holy of Holies where the presence of the Lord dwelt. As he stood there performing his priestly duties, I imagine he was praying. He was in the very presence of God at the moment Gabriel appeared. And when we pray, we too enter into communion with the One true God.

What are you doubting today? Do you need to hear the angel's message—fear not! Calm down! Don't rush about! Enjoy this holiday season! Spending some time in the presence of Jesus in prayer each morning will help you maintain a calm, relaxed focus during the season.

Today's Prayer

Lord, I don't want to be fearful or fretful. I want to trust You in all things and at all times. I want to enjoy this season that celebrates Your Son's birth. Keep me focused on You so that I can remain in Your presence moment by moment. I love You, Lord, amen.

Prepare My Heart

Write a note to Jesus today. Thank Him for His coming. Thank Him for helping you to live a life of faith rather than fear. Seal the note and place it on your tree or near your nativity to remind yourself to live a life of faith.

December 14
Stand In His Presence

Luke 1:18-23

And Zechariah said to the angel, "How shall I know this? For I am an old man, and my wife is advanced in years." And the angel answered him, "I am Gabriel. I stand in the presence of God, and I was sent to speak to you and to bring you this good news. And behold, you will be silent and unable to speak until the day that these things take place, because you did not believe my words, which will be fulfilled in their time." And the people were waiting for Zechariah, and they were wondering at his delay in the temple. And when he came out, he was unable to speak to them, and they realized that he had seen a vision in the temple. And he kept making signs to them and remained mute. And when his time of service was ended, he went to his home.

Unbelief! Zechariah simply could not believe the new—a baby after all these years. But this news, this news was coming straight from the one who stood in the presence of God. Yes, Gabriel actually had an audience with God on a regular basis. Can you imagine?

You and I have that opportunity on a daily basis as well. We can "stand in the presence of God" and delight in being near Him. We can come before Him in prayer, as we read the Word, or simply by communing with Him as we go about our day.

Today's Prayer

Precious Jesus, I desire to stand in Your presence daily. You are worthy of my devotion, and I love You. I ask for a greater glimpse of Your glory and majesty today and throughout this holiday season. Help me see You more clearly and help me believe You when You share truths from God that You have for me. In Jesus' name, amen.

Prepare My Heart

Do not neglect standing in the presence of the Lord this season. As a believer you are privileged to commune with the living God. Practice standing in the presence of the Lord today. As you go about your day, be conscience of His presence and remember Immanuel is with you.

December 15
Count Your Blessings

Luke 1:24-25
After these days his wife Elizabeth conceived, and for five months she kept herself hidden, saying, "Thus the Lord has done for me in the days when he looked on me, to take away my reproach among people."

"Thus the Lord has done for me." The news Elizabeth received, though shocking, was a tremendous blessing. She had waited years for a baby. So long that I'm sure she had begun to believe she would never be a mother. Yet she never acted as though she lost hope. She walked blamelessly before God in obedience to Him. I believe Elizabeth counted her blessings rather than her burdens. I believe she focused on the satisfaction that comes only from the Lord instead of the innermost longings of her heart.

"Thus the Lord has done for me." What has the Lord done for you? How has He totally amazed you this year? How has He blessed you? What are you waiting for Him to do? What have you asked of Him, even longed for Him to accomplish in your life? Have you allowed His presence to become your complete satisfaction?

Today's Prayer

Precious Jesus, the things You do for me are amazing. You bless me each and every day. Thank You for Your daily kindnesses. I praise You for the salvation that comes from You and the love that defines You. Teach me this coming year to find satisfaction in Your presence like never before, and to love You more each day. In Jesus' name, amen.

Prepare My Heart

I want to encourage you to make some lists today. Set aside ten minutes and write out things that God has done that have amazed and blessed you. Then, jot down ways you have seen yourself become more satisfied with Jesus than anything else. After you do this, pray and thank God for your list, then sit down with Him and have a cup of tea or cider and enjoy His presence for a few quiet moments. It will be His delight and yours!

December 16
The Favor of God

Luke 1:26-35

In the sixth month the angel Gabriel was sent from God to a city of Galilee named Nazareth, to a virgin betrothed to a man whose name was Joseph, of the house of David. And the virgin's name was Mary. And he came to her and said, "Greetings, O favored one, the Lord is with you!" But she was greatly troubled at the saying, and tried to discern what sort of greeting this might be. And the angel said to her, "Do not be afraid, Mary, for you have found favor with God. And behold, you will conceive in your womb and bear a son, and you shall call his name Jesus. He will be great and will be called the Son of the Most High. And the Lord God will give to him the throne of his father David, and he will reign over the house of Jacob forever, and of his kingdom there will be no end." And Mary said to the angel, "How will this be, since I am a virgin?" And the angel answered her, "The Holy Spirit will come upon you, and the power of the Most High will overshadow you; therefore the child to be born will be called holy—the Son of God.

The favor of God—what an inexplicable thought! To be favored is to be looked upon with delight, gladness, and joy. To be favored is to have the Lord with you. I want that! I want to experience and acknowledge the presence of the King of kings and

Lord of lords in my life each day.

Holy, perfect, complete, lacking nothing, set-apart, in full deity, God yet man—oh the depth of Jesus—our loving Lamb of God, Man of sorrows, Immanuel, God with us.

I love that He is holy, yet Immanuel. He is with us even though He is holy; because He is holy. Who else would choose to dwell with sinful creatures such as us other than our sweet, lovely Immanuel?

He is with us and for us, and He favors us. And as He favors us, He equips us to bear fruit for His Kingdom. As He favors us, we become like Him, because the influence He has on us changes and completes us. The favor of God. What a beautifully wrapped promise! His favor, His provision of grace, His great love.

Today's Prayer

Lord Jesus, come! Come and overshadow me with Your Holy Spirit. Grant me favor, gladness, joy, and delight from Your presence. Thank You for the beautifully wrapped promise of a Baby Boy who would bring good news of great joy to all. Thank You for this season of Advent. Thank You for the gift of Your presence. In Jesus' name, amen.

Prepare My Heart

Wrap a gift, bake a pie, make homemade cookies, do something fun and festive. As you do, think about who you can bless with your creation. Give the gift away in honor of our Savior who gave His all away for us.

December 17

Let It Be

Luke 1:36-38

And behold, your relative Elizabeth in her old age has also conceived a son, and this is the sixth month with her who was called barren. For nothing will be impossible with God." And Mary said, "Behold, I am the servant of the Lord; let it be to me according to your word." And the angel departed from her.

What in your life seems impossible today? Did you know that nothing is impossible with God? Yes, we "know" this information from a cerebral standpoint, but do we "know" it in our hearts? Do we take stock in it, stand on it, and believe it "even when" we don't see results?

Can you say, as Mary did after hearing this impossible news, "Behold, I am the servant of the Lord; let it be to me according to your word"? Let it be. These words express a deep truth in Mary's heart that we all need to grasp, "Even though what I see with our eyes seems impossible, I choose to believe. I choose to believe because of God." There is no need for any other reasoning, fretting, or explaining. God—just God.

Today's Prayer

Lord most holy, I praise You today for the reality of Your love and grace. I praise You for the reality of Your faithfulness and Your nature which is to embody truth and righteousness. Thank You for showing me Your power and the depth of Your love by making the impossible possible when You see fit. You are the God of possibilities. Let it be as You have said. I love You, Lord, amen.

Prepare My Heart

Make an impossible list today. Sit quietly and ask the Lord to show you the things on your heart and mind that you think are absolutely impossible. After making the list, tuck it into your Bible. Continue to pray about your impossible list and give thanks when God sees fit to make your impossible, possible.

December 18
Let Him Fill You

Luke 1:39-45
In those days Mary arose and went with haste into the hill country, to a town in Judah, and she entered the house of Zechariah and greeted Elizabeth. And when Elizabeth heard the greeting of Mary, the baby leaped in her womb. And Elizabeth was filled with the Holy Spirit, and she exclaimed with a loud cry, "Blessed are you among women, and blessed is the fruit of your womb! And why is this granted to me that the mother of my Lord should come to me? For behold, when the sound of your greeting came to my ears, the baby in my womb leaped for joy. And blessed is she who believed that there would be a fulfillment of what was spoken to her from the Lord."

What are you filled with this time of year? There is no room for an anxious heart when Jesus is in the room. Jesus filled Mary's womb with great joy and Elizabeth's with anticipation and delight. Do you allow Jesus' presence to replace your anxious thoughts with actions of love, kindness, and wonder?

Trust is key to letting go and letting God—Jesus in a manger—work through the details of your life. Try it today. Each time you begin to feel the stress of the calendar closing in (only 7 more days!!), think of Jesus, let go of your worry, and take delight in the Son of God.

Today's Prayer

Lord Jesus, You are the filler of my heart, the lover of my soul, the perfect, sinless, spotless lamb. Thank You for allowing me to sense Your presence and delight in Your love. Help me today to let go and let You fill me with peace, love, and joy. In Jesus' name, amen.

Prepare My Heart

Do you ever hear a song and then play it over and over in your mind? It's as though you can't get it out of your head. Let the Lord fill you with a song of joy today. Pause and sing, *Joy to the World.* As you go about your day, let that tune fill your heart, mind, and soul. Let His joy fill you!

December 19
A Song of Praise

Luke 1:46-56
And Mary said, "My soul magnifies the Lord, and my spirit rejoices in God my Savior, for he has looked on the humble estate of his servant. For behold, from now on all generations will call me blessed; for he who is mighty has done great things for me, and holy is his name. And his mercy is for those who fear him from generation to generation. He has shown strength with his arm; he has scattered the proud in the thoughts of their hearts; he has brought down the mighty from their thrones and exalted those of humble estate; he has filled the hungry with good things, and the rich he has sent away empty. He has helped his servant Israel, in remembrance of his mercy, as he spoke to our fathers, to Abraham and to his offspring forever." And Mary remained with her about three months and returned to her home.

Mary's Magnificat, a song of praise to her God. She was a blessed young woman, and her response to the favor and blessing of God? A heart overflowing with praise and worship. Notice the pronouns in her hymn of praise—*He, He, He. He* has done great things. *He* has brought down the mighty. *He* has filled the hungry. *He* has helped His servant. *He, He, He*. With her lips, eyes, hands, and heart she pointed her blessing back to God.

What a testimony of humility and love! Such a young girl, yet so wise and discerning. What is your Magnificat for Jesus? Your song of praise? What is in your heart today? Are you overwhelmed with a list of to-dos or are you overwhelmed with a list of praise and adoration for Jesus during this Advent?

Today's Prayer

Lord Jesus, You are the Savior of the world, the Prince of Peace, the Bright and Morning Star, King of kings and Lord of lords. You are worth everything to me. You are the reason I celebrate this season. Permeate my heart and mind with You today, Jesus. Help me focus on Your beauty and majesty in the midst of my hectic day. I magnify You, Lord. In Jesus' name, amen.

Prepare My Heart

Make a list today—not a to-do list. Make a list of the wonderful things about your Savior. Focus your list, not on the things He has done for you, but on who He is. Make this list a praise list!

December 20
And He Shall Be Called

Luke 1:57-66

Now the time came for Elizabeth to give birth, and she bore a son. And her neighbors and relatives heard that the Lord had shown great mercy to her, and they rejoiced with her. And on the eighth day they came to circumcise the child. And they would have called him Zechariah after his father, but his mother answered, "No; he shall be called John." And they said to her, "None of your relatives is called by this name." And they made signs to his father, inquiring what he wanted him to be called. And he asked for a writing tablet and wrote, "His name is John." And they all wondered. And immediately his mouth was opened and his tongue loosed, and he spoke, blessing God. And fear came on all their neighbors. And all these things were talked about through all the hill country of Judea, and all who heard them laid them up in their hearts, saying, "What then will this child be?" For the hand of the Lord was with him.

Oh the anticipation of the arrival of their son! After so many years of waiting, the time had arrived. A name was of great importance in their culture. There is always a significant meaning in a name. John was Elizabeth's choice and amazingly,

Zechariah's too. John—it's meaning in the Hebrew is so fitting—*Jehovah has been gracious*.

Jehovah had been gracious to this couple. He had answered their long-awaited prayer for a baby. In the fullness of time, God bent down and presented them with this gracious gift of love and kindness.

Do you show graciousness to others? Have you been kind and loving this Advent season? Are you displaying the gracious love of Christ to your neighbors, your co-workers, your family and friends?

Today's Prayer

Jehovah, Covenant Keeper, Master and Lord, thank You for the gift of salvation, the gift of mercy, the gift of peace in the midst of the storm. Thank You for giving me second chances. Thank You, for doing exceedingly, abundantly more than I could ever ask for or imagine! In Jesus' name, amen.

Prepare My Heart

What about you? Has Jehovah been gracious to you this year? Spend a few moments reflecting on God's grace in your life. Then think about these questions: If you had to name this year, what would you name it? Would it be the year of belief, of hope, of trust or bravery? Ponder this name today and ponder what you want next year's name to be.

December 21

Praise in the House

Luke 1:67-80

And his father Zechariah was filled with the Holy Spirit and prophesied, saying, "Blessed be the Lord God of Israel, for he has visited and redeemed his people and has raised up a horn of salvation for us in the house of his servant David, as he spoke by the mouth of his holy prophets from of old, that we should be saved from our enemies and from the hand of all who hate us; to show the mercy promised to our fathers and to remember his holy covenant, the oath that he swore to our father Abraham, to grant us that we, being delivered from the hand of our enemies, might serve him without fear, in holiness and righteousness before him all our days. And you, child, will be called the prophet of the Most High; for you will go before the Lord to prepare his ways, to give knowledge of salvation to his people in the forgiveness of their sins, because of the tender mercy of our God, whereby the sunrise shall visit us from on high to give light to those who sit in darkness and in the shadow of death, to guide our feet into the way of peace." And the child grew and became strong in spirit, and he was in the wilderness until the day of his public appearance to Israel.

"Prophet of the Most High." John, known to us as John the Baptist, the one who would prepare the way for Jesus, had come. And Zechariah's only response was praise. That really is the only proper response to God and His Son, Jesus. In all of our realities, Jesus shines forth like a beacon of hope and light bringing salvation, peace, forgiveness, mercy, loving-kindness, and blessings. What else could Zechariah's response have been for his son who would point others to One so precious? What is your response to Jesus' coming?

Today's Prayer

Jesus, You are Alpha and Omega, the Beginning and the End. You are the Righteous Counselor, Deliverer and Defender, the Faithful One, full of grace and truth, kind and merciful, powerful, sovereign, and in control. Thank You for coming, living a sinless life, and going to a cross for me so that I could be saved from a life without You. In Jesus' name, amen.

Prepare My Heart

Take time now to sit in Jesus' presence. Keep watch for ways you can help prepare the way for Jesus' coming for someone who doesn't know Him this season by pointing them to His goodness, grace, and love today.

December 22
Say 'Yes' to His Call

Matthew 1:18-25
Now the birth of Jesus Christ took place in this way. When his mother Mary had been betrothed to Joseph, before they came together she was found to be with child from the Holy Spirit. And her husband Joseph, being a just man and unwilling to put her to shame, resolved to divorce her quietly. But as he considered these things, behold, an angel of the Lord appeared to him in a dream, saying, "Joseph, son of David, do not fear to take Mary as your wife, for that which is conceived in her is from the Holy Spirit. She will bear a son, and you shall call his name Jesus, for he will save his people from their sins." All this took place to fulfill what the Lord had spoken by the prophet: "Behold, the virgin shall conceive and bear a son, and they shall call his name Immanuel" (which means, God with us). When Joseph woke from sleep, he did as the angel of the Lord commanded him: he took his wife, but knew her not until she had given birth to a son. And he called his name Jesus.

Fear! Fear often keeps us from doing what we know in our heart to be right. It paralyzes us, making us frozen and unable to obey. But God. God stepped in and spoke, assuring Joseph that this plan would change his life and the life of Mary, his betrothed. And Joseph? He faithfully trusted God, looked beyond his fear, and obeyed.

Joseph chose not to be concerned with the presumptions of others, the rumors and whispers. Instead He listened to the whisper of the Father. How sweet of God to speak to Joseph so tenderly in his dreams! What an honor to be chosen as the earthly father of the King of kings! God is so kind to use us to further the Kingdom. What has God asked you to do to help advance the Gospel recently? Will you, as Joseph did, say "yes" to God's call on your life?'

Today's Prayer

Precious Father, thank You for Your faithfulness. Thank You for trusting Your people to work alongside of You for the Kingdom. Help me to trust You at all times, even when things don't make sense. Give me eyes to see truth when it is unclear. Give me ears to hear Your voice speak and point me to the path of obedience. I love You, Lord, amen.

Prepare My Heart

Share the Gospel with someone. As the Lord leads tell your story of redemption to someone today.

December 23
Make Room for Empty

Philippians 2:5-7
Have this mind among yourselves, which is yours in Christ Jesus, who, though he was in the form of God, did not count equality with God a thing to be grasped, but emptied himself, by taking the form of a servant, being born in the likeness of men.

Servant Jesus lovingly came to us. Leaving His throne in Heaven, He came. Sacrificing His place on Heaven's throne for a time, He emptied Himself for humanity. Can you fathom such selflessness, such unconditional love, such generosity and mercy? Our Holy, Righteous, King Jesus gave up a portion of His deity to seek, serve, and save a lost mankind.

What have you sacrificed? What are you willing to give up in order to show love and kindness to others? How have you emptied yourself as a servant? Jesus' Advent ushered in emptiness—an empty throne at the right hand of God. But thanks be to God, Jesus' throne did not remain empty. He resides there and rules the nations with grace and love! Will you ask God to make room for "empty" in your life by giving you a sacrificial heart of love and generosity for others?

Today's Prayer

Precious Father, thank You for loving me. Thank Your for the gift of Your Son. Thank You, Jesus, for emptying Yourself for the world. Thank You for leaving Your throne room in Heaven so You could make a way for me. Help me be more like you, Jesus. Help me empty myself for others. I am eternally grateful for Your coming. I love You, Lord, amen.

Prepare My Heart

Pay it forward for someone today. In a drive-thru or at the grocery store or gas station, give a sacrificial gift to someone you don't know today.

December 24
The Word Made Flesh

John 1:14
And the Word became flesh and dwelt among us, and we have seen his glory, glory as of the only Son from the Father, full of grace and truth.

Jesus is the radiance of God's glory. HE IS full of grace and truth. HE IS the Word, the first born among creation, the Savior made flesh, the breath of God, come down from Heaven for you and me. HE CAME for you and me. And WE'VE SEEN His glory. Each and every time we seek Jesus' presence through a whispered prayer or the utterance of His Holy Word, His glory shines forth. His glory radiates every time we praise Him because He inhabits the praises of His people. We gain glimpses of His glory as we think about Him, and commune with Him, and feast on Him. HE IS the Word. God in flesh. God of glory.

Today's Prayer

Glory to God in the highest. Glory to God for the gift of His Son, Jesus. Glory to God for the gift of His presence, the gift of His Word, the gift of salvation and forgiveness. Glory to God! In the name of our glorious Jesus, amen.

Prepare My Heart

Meditate on John 1:14 and try your best to commit it to memory today. Let the Word dwell in your thoughts throughout the day.

December 25
Celebrate the King!

Luke 2:1-21
In those days a decree went out from Caesar Augustus that all the world should be registered. This was the first registration when Quirinius was governor of Syria. And all went to be registered, each to his own town. And Joseph also went up from Galilee, from the town of Nazareth, to Judea, to the city of David, which is called Bethlehem, because he was of the house and lineage of David, to be registered with Mary, his betrothed, who was with child. And while they were there, the time came for her to give birth. And she gave birth to her firstborn son and wrapped him in swaddling cloths and laid him in a manger, because there was no place for them in the inn. And in the same region there were shepherds out in the field, keeping watch over their flock by night. And an angel of the Lord appeared to them, and the glory of the Lord shone around them, and they were filled with great fear. And the angel said to them, "Fear not, for behold, I bring you good news of great joy that will be for all the people. For unto you is born this day in the city of David a Savior, who is Christ the Lord. And this will be a sign for you: you will find a baby wrapped in swaddling cloths and lying in a manger." And suddenly there was with the angel a multitude of the heavenly host praising God and saying, "Glory to God in the highest, and on earth peace among those with whom he is pleased!"

When the angels went away from them into heaven, the shepherds said to one another, "Let us go over to Bethlehem and see this thing that has happened, which the Lord has made known to us." And they went with haste and found Mary and Joseph, and the baby lying in a manger. And when they saw it, they made known the saying that had been told them concerning this child. And all who heard it wondered at what the shepherds told them. But Mary treasured up all these things, pondering them in her heart. And the shepherds returned, glorifying and praising God for all they had heard and seen, as it had been told them. And at the end of eight days, when he was circumcised, he was called Jesus, the name given by the angel before he was conceived in the womb.

He came! He came and all things changed. Jesus, precious Jesus, born baby—sinless, shameless, flawless, full of love and joy and peace. *He came!* The shepherds praised and believed. The angels sang. His mother and father worshiped this treasure from above. And we praise Him today. We lift our voices and sing of the joy, peace, and hope that came from His coming, *"Glory to God in the highest, and on earth peace among those with whom he is please!"*

Today's Prayer

Glory is Yours, Jesus. Thank You for coming. Thank You for a reason to celebrate this season. Help me treasure the experiences and joys of the season all year long. Help me bring glory to You each day. I take delight in You, Jesus, and I sing songs of praise to You this day! Amen.

Prepare My Heart

Sing a song of praise to the King today! Celebrate with joy the birth of our Savior, Jesus.

December 26

Forever Changed

Luke 2:22-35

And when the time came for their purification according to the Law of Moses, they brought him up to Jerusalem to present him to the Lord (as it is written in the Law of the Lord, "Every male who first opens the womb shall be called holy to the Lord") and to offer a sacrifice according to what is said in the Law of the Lord, "a pair of turtledoves, or two young pigeons." Now there was a man in Jerusalem, whose name was Simeon, and this man was righteous and devout, waiting for the consolation of Israel, and the Holy Spirit was upon him. And it had been revealed to him by the Holy Spirit that he would not see death before he had seen the Lord's Christ. And he came in the Spirit into the temple, and when the parents brought in the child Jesus, to do for him according to the custom of the Law, he took him up in his arms and blessed God and said, "Lord, now you are letting your servant depart in peace, according to your word; for my eyes have seen your salvation that you have prepared in the presence of all peoples, a light for revelation to the Gentiles, and for glory to your people Israel." And his father and his mother marveled at what was said about him And Simeon blessed them and said to Mary his mother, "Behold, this child is appointed for the fall and rising of many in Israel, and for a sign that is opposed (and a sword will pierce through your own soul also), so that thoughts from many hearts may be revealed."

It is impossible to encounter Jesus and not be changed. Many do not recognize the Holy One. Some ignore Him, some deny Him, some despise or dismiss Him. But for those who acknowledge Him, believe in Him, and turn to Him, they are forever changed for the better. Thanks be to God for this indescribable gift!

What changes have you seen in yourself through the Advent season as you have taken delight in Jesus? What does God want to change in you for the coming year?

Today's Prayer

Jesus, You are salvation; You came to save Your people. Thank You for saving me, blessing me, changing me. I ask that You continue to teach me what it means to know You, to know the salvation of the Lord. Help me to acknowledge Your presence in my life daily. I ask that You manifest Your presence in my heart each day, in Jesus' name, amen.

Prepare My Heart

Have you accepted Jesus into your heart? If not, have these past days of delighting in Him prepared your heart to experience Him personally? If so, stop and pray, asking Jesus to come into your heart, be your Lord and Savior and change your life forever. If you have already received Christ as Savior, will you pray today for someone you know who needs Jesus. Perhaps today is the day you are to share Jesus with this person.

December 27

A Woman of Worship

Luke 2:36-40

And there was a prophetess, Anna, the daughter of Phanuel, of the tribe of Asher. She was advanced in years, having lived with her husband seven years from when she was a virgin, and then as a widow until she was eighty-four. She did not depart from the temple, worshiping with fasting and prayer night and day. And coming up at that very hour she began to give thanks to God and to speak of him to all who were waiting for the redemption of Jerusalem. And when they had performed everything according to the Law of the Lord, they returned into Galilee, to their own town of Nazareth. And the child grew and became strong, filled with wisdom. And the favor of God was upon him.

Anna spent most of her life in the temple. Praying, fasting, waiting with hope, she knew the Messiah would come. And He came. He came and she recognized Him, praised, and proclaimed Him. She spoke of Him to all she encountered.

She was a part of changing the lives of those she encountered forever. A woman of worship and the Word, she must have studied the Scriptures diligently, being fully prepared, ready for His coming. And she recognized the Christ-child when she saw Him. There was no mistake. She knew.

What about you? Do you recognize the work of God around you? Do you know when He is speaking to you? Are you well-acquainted with the Scriptures because you spend quality time in the Word of God, gaining wisdom and knowledge? Do you proclaim the Lord to those with whom you come in contact?

Today's Prayer

Precious Jesus, thank You for leaving Your throne in heaven to come to earth. Thank You for emptying Yourself so that in receiving You, I might be made full. Help me proclaim You to those I encounter. Help me be bold and unafraid to spread the Good News of You. Give me the desire to study your Word daily so I can know You more and more. In Jesus' name, amen.

Prepare My Heart

Spend a few moments thinking about how you will study God's Word next year. Will you read through the Bible, journal a portion of Scripture daily, find a reading plan, or commit to a Bible study? Pray and ask God to give you wisdom to know what the best is for you at this age and stage of life.

December 28
Following Wisdom

Matthew 2:1-2
Now after Jesus was born in Bethlehem of Judea in the days of Herod the king, behold, wise men from the east came to Jerusalem, saying, "Where is he who has been born king of the Jews? For we saw his star when it rose and have come to worship him."

Wise men spent centuries seeking the One who was to redeem Israel. They devoted their lives to looking for Him. And finally, He came. A bright star led these wise men to the King of kings and Lord of lords. When they found Him, they worshipped.

What makes a person wise isn't schooling or breeding, and it isn't always knowing the right answers. Wisdom is much more at the core of who you are than that. Wisdom comes from knowing the One who is All-wise. Wisdom is seeking God's direction when you don't know the answers or the way you should go. Wisdom is found kneeling at the foot of the manger, in humility and fervency.

Are you a wise one? What do you spend your days doing? Are you looking to the Bright and Morning Star to show you the way? Are you following His lead?

Today's Prayer

Precious Jesus, King of kings and Lord of lords, Bright and Morning Star, Holy One, Promise Keeper, I praise You today. Thank You for showing me the way. Forgive me for looking to other things for guidance. Help me keep my eyes fixed on You. You know all the answers. Help me follow You and only You. In Jesus' name, amen.

Prepare My Heart

In what areas are you seeking wisdom for the upcoming year? Will you spend an extended time in prayer today, kneeling at the manager, asking for wisdom so you can know the way?

December 29
The Fullness of Time

Galatians 4:4-6
But when the fullness of time had come, God sent forth his Son, born of woman, born under the law, to redeem those who were under the law, so that we might receive adoption as sons. And because you are sons, God has sent the Spirit of his Son into our hearts, crying, "Abba! Father!" So you are no longer a slave, but a son, and if a son, then an heir through God.

"In the fullness of time." What a wonderful phrase! So much promise, hope, and security rests in those few words of extravagant love. I am grateful for "the fullness of time," aren't you? In the fullness of time—Jesus. Jesus came. Love, overflowing from a manger, came for you and for me. Redemption, seeping through the blanket of a beautiful baby boy whose purpose was to ransom mankind laid waiting, longing to restore and rescue.

Today's Prayer

Precious Jesus, I am so thankful that through You, I am an heir to God. Because You came, lived, died, rose from the dead, and sent the Holy Spirit, I can call God my Father. Thank You! Thank You for coming and living and loving. Thank You for teaching and training and leading. Thank You for being patient, kind, and merciful even when I fail. In Your name I pray, amen.

Prepare My Heart

Time is such a commodity. Set aside time today or sometime before the end of the year to examine this past year. What goals did you accomplish? How have you grown in your spiritual journey? What is God whispering to you about the new year? Has He given you any new goals? Make a plan for the new year. Write out what the Lord is telling you so that you can be fully prepared for the time you will spend in the upcoming days of this new year dawning.

December 30

Prince and Savior

Acts 5:31

God exalted him to his own right hand as Prince and Savior that he might bring Israel to repentance and forgive their sins.

Ponder those words. Prince and Savior. Contemplate what that means. Jesus is Prince and Savior. As Prince He is our sovereign ruler. As Savior He is our refuge, our life boat, the One who rescues us.

Ruler and Refuge—God is both at the same time. What an unfathomable truth. Powerful yet near, in charge yet caring and gracious. How does this knowledge affect you? How does remembering that Jesus is your Prince and Savior help you as you go about your day and prepare for the up-coming new year?

Today's Prayer

Thank You, Father, for exalting Your Son as Prince and Savior. Thank You for the confidence, hope, and redemption His Lordship brings. Help me look to You, Jesus, as I face my day. Remembering who You are, and the power You possess, gives me security. I love You, Lord, amen.

Prepare My Heart

What in this next year needs to be released from your hands? What has God called you to do that causes you to fear? Will you take refuge in Him? Literally, (as a symbol of surrender) open your hands to the Father and resign control over your biggest fear. Then read the Scripture below as a prayer, asking God to help you

Fear not, for I am with you; be not dismayed, for I am your God; I will strengthen you, I will help you, I will uphold you with my righteous right hand.
—Isaiah 41:10

December 31
Every Knee Should Bow

Philippians 2:8-10
And being found in human form, he humbled himself by becoming obedient to the point of death, even death on a cross. Therefore God has highly exalted him and bestowed on him the name that is above every name, so that at the name of Jesus every knee should bow, in heaven and on earth and under the earth, and every tongue confess that Jesus Christ is Lord, to the glory of God the Father.

Christ. He humbled Himself, came, lived, and died. All for you and for me. But God. God raised Jesus from the dead. Jesus is exalted above all, crowned in glory forever! Confess that today. Confess His glory and majesty and power. Bow before Him. Bow to Him in humble adoration, giving thanks for this season of Advent—the celebration of His coming.

Today's Prayer

Jesus, You are exalted, high and lifted up. I praise You as Alpha and Omega, the Beginning and the End. You were at the beginning of this year and You are at the end, and You are everything in between. I ask that You permeate my days throughout the coming year with the peace of Your presence. Fill me with joy in Your presence as we walk out this new year together. Praising You Jesus! Amen.

Prepare My Heart

Sit with Jesus today. Sit. Have a cup of tea or coffee and reflect on December. Did you find delight each day as you took time to think about the season of Christ's birth? Journal your thoughts. Write out what this season has meant to you and taught you. Give thanks to the Father for His precious Son, Jesus.

About the Author

With a passion for God's Word, practical insights, and in-depth teaching, Jacqueline leads her audiences, big or small, in person or in prose to look to God for the answers to life's most difficult questions.

Jacqueline loves studying and teaching God's Word and finds endless joy and blessing in leading women into a deeper, more passionate relationship with Jesus Christ and encouraging them to know God and seek His purpose for their lives.

The Lord called Jacqueline into full-time ministry in 2006. Currently, she is on staff at Warren Baptist Church as the Director of Women's Ministry, Prayer, and Resource Writer. Because of her love for teaching the Word of God and spreading the Gospel, Jacqueline has led many retreats and conferences in the U.S. and abroad. Jacqueline loves to write and several of her articles were published in *Faith Magazine* throughout 2013-2014.

You can experience every day life with Jacqueline on her blog at *jacquelineheider.com*. When she's not writing or speaking, you can find her riding horses, watching movies, eating, reading, going to the beach, hanging out or shopping with friends, and most often spending time with her favorite people—her husband Alex, and their three children.